PORTUGAL

A Travellers' Guide

PORTUGAL

A Travellers' Guide

SUSAN LOWNDES

THORNTON COX

Distribution:
Distributed in Great Britain and the Commonwealth by
Roger Lascelles, 47 York Road, Brentford, Middlesex TW8 0QP
Telephone: 01-847-0935

ISBN 0 902726 42 0

Distributed in the United States and Canada by
Hippocrene Books Inc., 171 Madison Avenue, New York NY 10016

US ISBN 0 87052 720 7
Distributed in Portugal by Dinternal, Rua da Gloria 8,
1298 Lisboa Codex

Published by Thornton Cox (1986) Ltd,
Epworth House,
23-35 City Road, London EC1Y 1AA

Published in the United States and Canada
by Hippocrene Books Inc., 171 Madison Avenue, New York, NY 10016

First published by Geographia Ltd 1982. Second Edition, fully
revised, January 1987. Third edition 1989

Drawings by Guy Magnus
Maps by Tom Stalker-Miller, MSIA
Series editor: Kit Harding

Cover: Albufeira. Photograph J. Allan Cash
Colour photographs on pages 103 and 104 by courtesy
Portuguese National Tourist Office. Photograph on
page 101 (lower) by Peter Wilson. All other photographs
by Richard Cox.

*Great care has been taken throughout this book to be accurate,
but the publishers cannot accept responsibility for any errors
which appear*

Printed in Great Britain by The Guernsey Press Company Limited,
Guernsey, Channel Islands. Set in 8½ on 9½ pt Univers

Thornton Cox Guides:

Titles in print in this series include:

Egypt	**Ireland**
Southern France	**Kenya**
Greece	**Majorca**

Titles being prepared include:

Malta	**Southern Spain**
Southern Africa	**Northern & Central Spain**

Lagos in the Algarve

Contents

Author's Acknowledgments
I am grateful to Senhora D. Maria Luisa Matos Ferreira who came with me to explore the Algarve, to my daughter Ana Marques Vicente who made helpful suggestions, and to Senhor Luis Custodio of the Portuguese Tourist Office in London, who arranged for me to visit the north again and stay in several *pousadas*.

I would also like to acknowledge my indebtedness in the writing of this book, not only to Mrs W. D. Thorburn, who has typed and retyped with the greatest patience and added much to my knowledge of Tras-os-Montes, where she was brought up, but to the staffs of the many local tourist offices who eagerly answered my questions, to the custodians of museums, who communicated to me their pride and pleasure in the objects under their care, and to the caretakers who so amiably unlocked remote churches and monasteries for me.

The Author
Susan Lowndes has lived in Portugal for many years and knows the country intimately. In addition to the books listed below, she has written many articles on Portugal for British and American publications and is the Correspondent of an American News Agency.

The daughter of F. S. A. Lowndes of THE TIMES and Marie Belloc Lowndes the novelist, and a niece of Hilaire Belloc, Susan Lowndes is the widow of a Portuguese writer and foreign Correspondent, Luiz Marques, who owned and edited THE ANGLO-PORTUGUESE NEWS, which she carried on after his death, selling it some time ago.

By the same author

THE SELECTIVE TRAVELLER IN PORTUGAL
(with Ann Bridge)

GOOD FOOD FROM SPAIN AND PORTUGAL

LETTERS OF MARIE BELLOC LOWNDES
(edited)

Foreword

Portugal, cut off from the rest of the continent by the great land mass of Spain and bounded on the west and south by the Atlantic Ocean, is the westernmost country of continental Europe. Its relatively small area of 34,207 sq. miles (88,551 sq. kms) falls gradually down from the more mountainous terrain on the frontier to the valleys of the four main rivers, the Tagus, the Douro, the Mondego and the Sado and the flatter country by the sea.

Until comparatively recently, Portugal was virtually unknown to travellers. Now more and more people are coming to this country which has an astonishing variety of landscape and of fine architecture, as well as unparalleled beaches on its long indented coastline. There are mercifully few motorways, so the motorist not only should, but must, take his time in getting around.

With the exceptions of Lisbon with around a million inhabitants, and Oporto with 400,000, the population of almost ten million is mainly concentrated in the north and centre of the country, the Algarve and the Alentejo being far more sparsely populated. Widespread emigration to France and Germany, and to a lesser degree to Brazil, has been mostly from the north, Minho, Tras-os-Montes, Douro and the Beiras. The effects of this can be seen in the prosperity of even remote villages, for the emigrants almost always return to their *terra,* their native soil, with the money they have prudently saved, and rebuild their houses.

The Portuguese are kindly and easy-going, and preserve many old-fashioned values which have disappeared in other countries. Family life is important, the aged are respected and children take a full part in the life of their parents and siblings.

The country is divided into provinces. From north to south, these are: the Minho, highly cultivated and wooded; Tras-os-Montes (literally Over-the-Hills), in the extreme north-eastern corner of the country, is mainly a high plateau where sheep graze; sweet chestnut and walnut trees flourish on the lower slopes, and vines on the steep terraces falling down to the river Douro in the south provide the grapes for port wine.

The Douro is the smallest province, surrounding Oporto and much like the Minho in its level of cultivation and numerous villages. It is in this part of the country that there are the most important Iron Age remains as well as a plethora of early Christian churches. The Beiras, Litoral (Coastal), Alta (Upper) and Baixa (Lower), stretch from the Atlantic right across to the Spanish frontier. The Beira Litoral below

Foreword

Oporto, is cut by rivers and waterways and is one of the main rice-growing regions, particularly along the lower reaches of the Mondego below the ancient University city of Coimbra. The Beira Alta and the Beira Baixa are the most mountainous regions of the country, with the Serra da Estrela cutting across from north east to south west, and other lesser ranges. The lower slopes of these mountains are covered with wooded plantations, the summits rocky with occasional pasturage for sheep. Lakes, some artificial, lighten the austere country and provide irrigation for small plots of fertile land.

The Mondego valley, east of Coimbra, consists of rich arable land and vineyards in the Dão region from which the well-known wine takes its name. The valley of the river Zezere rises to the Cova da Beira, famous for sheep and the main wool producing part of the country. Many of the towns and villages are fortified against the traditional enemy — Spain. The houses are of granite and seem to sink into the bare landscape of the upper reaches.

Estremadura, running up the coast from Lisbon to Leiria and south to Setúbal, is undulating and cultivated, the land nearer to Lisbon supplying most of the fruit and vegetables for the capital. The few ranges of low hills include those on which the Lines of Torres Vedras were erected in the Peninsular War to protect Lisbon; the Serra de Sintra, to the west of the capital; and the Serra da Arrábida to the south of the Tagus, which falls down to the river Sado.

Up river from Lisbon lies the Ribatejo, the rich riverine plain with rice fields, market gardens and great pastures on which splendid horses and black fighting bulls roam freely. Santarem, a leading agricultural centre, is the main city of this province. The smaller towns and villages are prosperous and busy and many of the *'campinos'* or herdsmen, still wear their traditional dress of black breeches, white stockings, red waistcoats and stocking caps.

The Alentejo occupies nearly a third of the total land area of the country and lies between the Atlantic Ocean and Spain. The province is flat, with every eminence crowned by a castle-topped whitewashed village or town. Vast wheatfields stretch into the shimmering distance and groves of olive trees and cork oaks provide the only shade. Herds of razor-backed black pigs root around for acorns and provide the delicious fresh and cured pork for which the Alentejo is famous. Low hills run up to the Spanish frontier, along which are remote and isolated fortified villages, some now utterly deserted, as well as the large and prosperous cities of Elvas, Estremoz and Portalegre. Evora is the lovely, unspoilt capital of the Upper Alentejo; Beja, now industrialised, of the Lower. Numerous dams and irrigation projects have rendered the dry land more fertile, as they have in the southern-most province, the Algarve.

The Algarve is now the best known part of Portugal for the visitor. The sandy beaches are endless, clean and safe on the southern coast, the few to the west sometimes getting the full force of the Atlantic. Inland there are many interesting and beautiful places and Faro, the capital is one of the most fascinating cities in Portugal.

Tourist complexes, hotels and restaurants, and the water sports centres where a whole day can be spent on the huge slides and other water-based amusements with ample room for sunbathing, swimming in the large pools and eating in the cafeterias are mercifully confined to the main resorts. In between there are still almost deserted beaches and inlets of the sea, reached by narrow side-roads, often unsignposted, so visitors with a car or strong walkers can have a rewarding holiday discovering these remote and unknown places.

The province is separated from the Alentejo by a range of low hills which effectively cut it off from the rest of the country for many centuries. So it is here that there still exist many traces of the Moorish occupation, not only in the numerous place names beginning Al, but also in the architecture and customs. The roofs of houses are often flat as in Olhão, the chimneys fretted in Arabic designs and the older country people dress in dark clothing to protect them from the sun.

General Information

How to get there

By Air
Portugal's national airline TAP, Air Portugal, has daily services to most European capitals from Lisbon, Faro and Oporto. British Airways also flies daily to these cities and several lines fly from British provincial airports and from Gatwick.

Transatlantic flights are operated by TAP and TWA to and from New York, and TAP and Canadian Pacific cover Toronto and Montreal. Most airlines have fly/drive arrangements at reasonable cost, which are worth looking into as it is sometimes impossible to hire a car on arrival in the country. Package tours with hotel and breakfast, or half or full board included, are sometimes cheaper than the ordinary return air fare. There are no special buses to and from the Airports, though ordinary buses run from Lisbon Airport into various areas of the city, taking about 40 minutes. Taxis take about 20 minutes and are cheap compared with London or New York.

By Sea
There are now no regular sailings between Lisbon and either the UK or North America. Brittany Ferries run a direct route from Plymouth to Santander in Northern Spain, which is the quickest way to take your own car to Portugal and avoids the long haul down through France and across Spain.

Frontier posts with Spain are generally open from 0700 to 0100. But those at Caia, Vilar Formoso, Vila Verde da Raia and Valença do Minho do not close at all in the summer months or at Christmas and Easter.

By Rail
The 'Sud' express runs daily from Paris to Lisbon with 2nd class couchettes and 1st class sleepers, though those taking the latter have to change at Irun on the French/Spanish frontier. There is a restaurant car and for those who enjoy leisurely rail travel the 26 hours in the train are well spent. Some trains take cars from Paris to Lisbon daily in the summer, once a week in winter.

Travel within the Country

Air
Regular daily air services connect Lisbon with Oporto and Faro. Some country towns are linked to the capital by small aircraft.

Rail
There is a good railway network over the country which is very reasonable in price. Travellers with a Rail Europ card pay half the basic fare. The only express trains are those between Sta Apolonia Station in Lisbon and Oporto, four slower trains each day take cars for a modest price. Passengers can travel on a different train to that on which their car travels and pick it up when they like at their destination. Trains can be very crowded so it is wise to buy your 1st or 2nd class ticket in advance and get a reserved place. For passengers the Lisbon/Algarve line starts at Barreiro, on the south side of the river Tagus, reached by ferry from the Sul e Leste Station at Praça do Comercio. There are minor lines from Oporto to Tras-os-Montes which are slow but scenically rewarding, especially the one which goes up the Douro to Barca de Alva on the Spanish frontier.

One of the other most picturesque lines is that from Lisbon to Guarda via Abrantes. Shortly after passing the romantic castle of Almourol on an island in the Tagus, the train follows the river for some 40 miles on a single track line cut out of the side of the hills. There are no roads, the slopes are sparsely cultivated, olive trees perch on what look like inaccessibly steep bluffs, rare birds swoop and dive and the colour of the water below is changed by the springs which feed it.

Frequent electric trains link Cais do Sodré station in Lisbon, with Estoril, Cascais and the other resorts on the Sunny Coast. Another electric line goes to Sintra from the Rossio Station in Lisbon. It is essential to buy your ticket before starting as, if bought on the train, there is a *very* heavy surcharge.

Road
Traffic keeps to the right, vehicles entering roads from the right have priority, unless there is a Stop sign at the junction. There are very few motorways. Most roads are well surfaced, but narrow and twisting. The Portuguese are notoriously bad drivers and take appalling risks. In the north there are still bullock-drawn carts and people riding mules and donkeys. Pedestrians are apt to walk in the centre of roads both in the towns and in the country.

Buses
Bus services cover every part of the country and long-distance lines

General Information

link Lisbon with the Algarve, Oporto and other places. Lisbon, Oporto and Coimbra have bus and tram services — bus stops have signs marked *Paragem* — and Lisbon also has an underground train system.

Taxis

Taxis run on meters and are cheap by international standards. The driver has a right to charge for the return journey if taken outside the town boundaries, and 20 percent more from 2200 to 0600. A tip of about 10 percent of the fare is normal. Taxis are instantly recognised by their green roofs and black bodies.

Car Hire

Avis, Contauto, Hertz, InterRent and most international firms have offices at Lisbon, Faro and Oporto airports, as well as many local firms. It is wise to hire your self-drive car before arrival as there is a great run on these cars in the high season. Visitors bringing their own cars should have a valid British, American or international driving licence, international car insurance (green card), and nationality plates, as well as a luminous triangle for use when a car is immobilised on the highway. Spare parts are available. The Portuguese Automobile Club is the Automovel Clube de Portugal, Rua Rosa Araujo 24-26, 1200 Lisbon. Fuel prices are among the highest in Europe. Seat belts are obligatory.

Where to stay

Hotels, Pousadas

Local tourist offices have lists of hotels and boarding houses in every category. Some of the luxury hotels are superb and the Government sponsored *Pousadas* are often located in converted castles and fine old houses. All rooms have baths and the food in the restaurants is usually excellent. Prices include all taxes and service charges. For a list of *Pousadas* see page 175.

Country Houses

Turismo de Habitação, or Country House accommodation, is the name by which a number of private houses receive paying guests in conditions of great comfort. The majority of these are in the north, and are often beautiful manor houses. Prices for double room and breakfast start at around 7,000$00, and simple dinners can be provided on request from 1,500$00 to 3,000$00 for several courses. A selection of these country houses will be included in each chapter, but complete particulars can be obtained from Avenida Antonio Augusto de Aguiar 86-3 1000 Lisbon (tel. 575493) or call Ponte de Lima 058-942335 for houses in the north.

Estalagems, Residencias, Pensions

Estalagems are privately run tourist inns and are often located in towns, as are *Residencias* which only serve breakfast. But every town in Portugal has reasonable restaurants. *Pensões* or boarding houses are very good value, though it is rare to get a private bathroom. Portugal is a very clean country and even in Lisbon and large towns, housewives hang out their wash to dry from struts attached to window sills or balconies, regardless of passers-by, so even the humblest pension is usually clean and neat.

Camping and Hostels
There are good camping sites and youth hostels all over the country, particulars from the tourist offices. There is a certain freedom of parking for caravans, as there are not too many.

Holiday Homes
Holiday homes rented for short periods are almost unknown outside the Algarve. There they form a major business, and all the main agents abroad have their correspondents in the Algarve who supply full particulars, arrange for visitors to be met at Faro Airport by a self-drive car, and see there is food in the refrigerator for the first meal. The services of cleaning women, who come in every morning, are included in the rent.

Banks and Currency
Banking hours are from 0830 to 1500. Closed on Saturdays. The unit of currency is the escudo, with the dollar sign between the escudo and the centavos. Thus, 105$50 is one hundred and five escudos and fifty centavos. The rate of exchange varies and a better rate is to be had at banks than in hotels or shops. One pound sterling is equal to approximately 250 escudos. Travellers cheques in sterling or dollars are the safest way to carry money. Notes of 5,000$00, 1,000$00, 500$00 and 100$00 are in circulation, as are coins of 50$00, 25$00, 20$00, 10$00, 5$00, 2$50 and 1$00.

Churches
There is no state religion in Portugal but the vast majority of the population is Roman Catholic, so there are Catholic churches with Mass on Sundays in every town and village.

The Church of England has churches in Lisbon, Estoril, Oporto, and the Algarve. These are St George's, St Paul's, St James's and St Vincent's respectively.

The Irish Dominican Order has served the Catholic church of Corpo Santo in Lisbon for over 300 years. Masses in English on Sundays and weekdays. On Sundays in St Sebastian's Chapel in Cascais, and in São Pedro do Estoril. Various other bodies have churches or meeting places which are listed under *Igreja,* in the telephone directories.

Clubs and Libraries

The Royal British Club, Rua da Estrela 8, 1200 Lisbon, is mainly a lunch club. The American Women of Lisbon have a Club house in Cascais at Avenida de Sintra 3, offering meals and various activities. The Anglo-American Library is on the premises, open three mornings a week. The British Institute, Rua Luis Fernandes 3, 1200 Lisbon, has an excellent library and reading room, open daily except Wednesday mornings, and the American Library, under the auspices of the US Embassy, at Avenida Duque de Loulé 22-B, 1000 Lisbon, is open every afternoon.

Consulates

Australia: Avenida da Liberdade 244-4, 1200 Lisbon; tel. 523350.
Canada: Rua Rosa Araujo 2-6, 1200 Lisbon; tel. 563821.
New Zealand: New Zealand interests are looked after by the British Consulate.
UK: Rua São Domingos à Lapa 37, 1200 Lisbon; tel. 661191.
USA: Avenida das Forças Armadas, 1600 Lisbon; tel. 7266600.

Customs and Immigration

The regulations for Customs and Immigration are similar to those in other EEC countries, but it is always wise to check with your travel agent as they may be changed from time to time.

Visitors are allowed to bring in reasonable personal possessions, such as a camera, radio, jewellery and so on. Duty free allowances are 200 cigarettes, or ½ lb tobacco, two litres of wine and one litre of spirits.

The maximum amount of Portuguese currency permitted to be brought in or taken out is restricted. It is advisable to check with your travel agent.

No visas are required for American or British passport holders, nor for visitors from EEC countries. But if you are staying for more than 60 days you must apply for permission to do so. Health certificates are not required.

Dress

The sun can be dangerously hot in the summer and it is not safe to be a long time on the beach without a shady hat. When it rains, which is rare in the six summer months, it comes down with tropical intensity and the temperature falls after sunset, so even in the summer it is wise to bring a light coat. (Snow is almost unknown, as are heavy frosts in winter.) Low heeled, comfortable shoes are essential for walking in Lisbon, or any other town or village, as pavements are usually made up of mosaics of tiny stones and even in the north, where the paving stones are of granite, they are seldom kept evenly laid. In short, dress for both men and women is much the same as in any other warm southern country.

Etiquette

The Portuguese are a formal people and good manners will get the visitor anywhere. Shake hands with your hairdresser, hotel porter and indeed anyone who has been especially helpful. Visitors always turn round to say a final farewell before disappearing from view. The words *'com licença'*, 'allow me', are a great help if for instance you find all the tables occupied in a café, and want to sit in a vacant chair, or have to push past anyone in a crowd.

Festivals and Entertainment

Romarias or religious festivals, are held to honour the local patron saint in countless towns and villages. The most famous pilgrimage centre in the whole Iberian peninsula is that of Fatima, 90 miles north of Lisbon, where huge crowds of pilgrims gather on the 13th of each month from May to October to commemorate the apparitions of the Virgin to three shepherd children there in 1917.

Country fairs are always held in connection with *romarias,* and most country towns have their regular weekly or monthly market of fatstock and produce.

The Calouste Gulbenkian Foundation has done much to bring music and ballet into the provinces, with special festivals held in different cities during the summer, in addition to the winter and spring programmes at the headquarters in Lisbon, and the summer season in Estoril and the Costa do Sol.

The latest films are shown in all cinemas and Portuguese TV relies heavily on imported programmes.

Casinos with roulette, chemin de fer, baccarat and slot machines are at Estoril near Lisbon, Alvor, Monte Gordo and Vilamoura in the Algarve, Figueira da Foz near Coimbra and Espinho and Póvoa de Varzim on the Costa Verde in the north. Visitors must take their passports.

Food and Wine

The Portuguese eat food that is in season, as frozen and packaged food is far more expensive than fresh food. Fish is superb, but dear apart from fresh sardines. Fruit and vegetables are excellent when carefully chosen; all shopkeepers allow customers to feel fruit and vegetables and even fish. Battery chickens have only started to be produced recently so most poultry is well flavoured. Beef is apt to be tough; pork both fresh and in its many smoked forms is excellent; lamb and mutton have to be chosen with care as they tend to be scraggy. Every part of Portugal has its local cheese, usually made from ewe's or goat's milk. The best known are the *Queijo da Serra,* from the Estrela mountains, like a softer type of *Brie. Azeitão,* from near Setúbal is somewhat similar. *Ilha* or *São Jorge* is a type of Cheddar from the Azores Islands and is excellent for cooking. The small *Queijos Frescos* and *Requeijão,* made from goat's milk curds, should be eaten fresh to capture the real flavour. Most produce is considerably cheaper in local markets which are in every town and village, than in shops or supermarkets.

Some of the best wines in Portugal are purely local, such as Buçaco near Coimbra, Nabantino in Tomar, Vidigueira, Borba, Evel, Redondo in the Alentejo, Lagoa and Tavira in the Algarve. But these local wines are gradually becoming available in Lisbon and other cities, and if you are eating in a restaurant with a wine list look out for the more unfamiliar names. Some of the better known wines come from the Dão and Colares regions. Red and white, rosés such as Mateus, and the green *(vinho verde),* slightly petillant wines from the north are on most wine lists. In more modest eating houses ask for the *vinho da casa,* that is the house wine; it is almost always good, either red, *tinto,* or white, *branco.*

Sagres is the best known name in lager and beer and there are other good types of foreign beers.

Port is little drunk in its country of origin, but is available in most places. White port is taken as an aperitif before meals and the heavier reds, tawny, crusted and vintage come in all the famous names. There is a fascinating Port Wine Institute in Lisbon, open from 1000 to midnight, at Rua S. Pedro de Alcantara 45, where there are 200 varieties to be tasted. Madeira is a drier, more sherry-like wine and there is a delicious sweet Muscatel from Setúbal.

Portuguese brandy can be very good, as is the local gin. Vodka, and every type of liqueur, is imitated and is very much less expensive than imported spirits. Whisky, however, cannot be imitated and genuine Scotch can be bought in all good grocers and supermarkets, cheaper than in England as the duty is much lower.

Gratuities

Tips are now included in hotel and restaurant bills, but an extra five to ten percent is acceptable and wise if you intend to return. Porters expect 100$00 a piece of luggage or more if there are very few, theatre ushers and/cloakroom girls 100$00. Men give 100$00 in barbershops and women 100$00 or more according to the services rendered. Museum custodians receive 100$00 to 200$00 and more if a party is taken round. Taxi drivers should get around 10% of the fare.

Language

Portuguese is easy to read by anyone with even a slight knowledge of Spanish, French or Italian. However it is difficult to pronounce and hard to understand as people speak quickly and elliptically. Vowels with a tilde (ã) over them are nasalized, and words ending with N or M sound as if they end with a G; eng, bong etc. The cedilla (ç) transforms the C into an SS sound as in French, and an acute accent, indicates a syllabic stress. Words ending in a vowel are usually pronounced with the stress on the next to last syllable, those ending with consonants have the stress on the last syllable.

Useful phrases

Good morning	Bom dia
Good afternoon	Boa tarde
Good evening	Boa noite
Goodbye	Adeus
Please	Sé faz favor
Thank you	Obrigado
Many thanks	Muito obrigado
To the right	À direita
To the left	À esquerda
Bus or tram stop	Paragem
Today	Hoje
Tomorrow	Amanha
Where is the hotel?	Onde é o hotel?
Restaurant	Restaurante or tasca
Breakfast	Pequeno almoço
Lunch	Almoço
Dinner	Jantar
Tea	Chá
Coffee	Café
Tourist Office	Turismo
How much does this cost?	Quanto custa?
Forgive me	Desculpe-me
What time is it?	Que horas são?
I don't understand	Não entendo
W.C./Bathroom	Toilete/casa de banho
Men	Homens
Women	Senhoras
Bus	Autocarro
Train	Comboio

Lavatories

There are public lavatories in all museums and railway stations, as well as in special small buildings or below ground in towns. Visitors should look out for the signs *Senhoras* (women) or *Homens* (men).

Medical Services

The Portuguese National Health Service has improved greatly of recent years and a reciprocal agreement exists between the British and Portuguese Services, though not every hospital knows this fact. Many doctors and specialists have done post-graduate work in Great Britain or the United States, so English-speaking doctors are not difficult to find. There is a British Hospital with English-speaking nurses and doctors, at Rua Saraiva de Carvalho 49, 1200 Lisbon, tel. 602020, with a daily Out-Patients department, two small wards and several single rooms. All State hospitals have emergency out-patient services.

Museums

Normally open from 1000 to midday and from 1400 to 1700 every day except Monday. Entrance fees vary but are usually between 150$00 and 300$00, sometimes free on Saturdays and Sundays. Palaces are closed on Tuesdays.

Office hours

These are open from 0930 or 1000 to 1730 or 1800 with a break for lunch. Post Offices have the same opening hours, with the exception of the main Offices which remain open during lunch. The one in the Restauradores in Lisbon is open 24 hours.

Public Holidays

New Year's Day (January 1), Carnival (Tuesday before Ash Wednesday), Good Friday (moveable), anniversary of the 1974 Revolution (April 25), Labour Day (May 1), National Day (June 10), Corpus Christi (moveable), Assumption (August 15), First Republic (October 5), All Saints (November 1), Restoration (December 1), Immaculate Conception (December 8), Christmas Day (December 25).

Restaurants

It is rare to find badly cooked food in a restaurant. The best restaurants are very good and much less dear than their counterparts in the UK. There is a wide range of middle-priced places with dishes at around 750$00, but the portions are so large that few eat more than one course and it is customary for three people to share two portions of an entrée and of the main course. Cheap restaurants called *tascas,* can be distinguished from taverns by the fact that they have tablecloths and food is not served on marble or plastic-topped tables. The food is rough but well flavoured. Meal times are later than in the UK or USA. Lunch seldom starts before 1300 to 1330 and dinner before 2000.

Cafés and pastrycooks are everywhere and often serve simple meals of ham and eggs or meat pasties or rissoles. Cakes are sweet and rich, sometimes with nuts and eggs incorporated.

Shopping

Opening hours vary greatly; shops in commercial centres are often open all day, and on Sundays, until 2300 or midnight. However, the better shops still open at 0900, close for lunch from 1300 to 1500, then open until 1900. In the north the lunchtime closing is more usually from midday to 1400. All these shops are closed from 1300 on Saturdays and all day on Sundays. The best buys are the local craftsmanship — basketwork, lace, embroidery, leather, filigree jewellery, copperware, pottery, porcelain, glazed tiles, cork, local textiles, carpets, musical instruments, marble and woodwork.

Spas

Portugal is rich in Spas, recommended for a variety of complaints. These thermal waters are now coming back into fashion and for certain rheumatic complaints they are unrivalled. The better known Spas all have good hotels, full of old world charm. The best for rheumatism are at Caldas da Rainha and the Termas dos Cucos, with natural hot mud baths, near Torres Vedras, both not far from Lisbon, and Caldas de Monchique in the Algarve. For digestive troubles and kidney complaints, Luso and Curia, near Aveiro, Vidago and Pedras Salgadas, in the north, Montfortinho, near Castelo Branco, and Vimeiro, north of Lisbon, are all highly thought of. There are sulphur baths for asthma and bronchitis at Entre-os-Rios, near Oporto, and circulatory troubles are said to be improved at Caldelas, near Braga, where the waters have the same mineral content as those at Bad Kissingen in Bavaria.

Sport

Almost every beach in Portugal is wide and sandy. Those in the Algarve are particularly good, with safer swimming than those on the west coast, where the heavy Atlantic rollers can be a serious hazard, though warnings are issued when this is the case. It is therefore wiser to bathe from a beach with a Guard and bathing is forbidden when it is considered to be dangerous. The beaches on the estuary of the Tagus are apt to be polluted. Nude bathing is not usual and is confined to a few beaches in the Algarve and on the Costa da Caparica, south of Lisbon.

Bullfighting

The Portuguese bullfight is entirely different from the Spanish version. The bull is not killed and he is fought by superb horsemen called *cavaleiros,* on magnificent stallions, which are as highly trained as polo ponies. The *toureiros,* on foot, first engage the bull with skilled cape work, before the rider enters the fray and, as the bull charges again and again, places a dart in the thick muscles of the beast's huge neck. Finally, when the bull is tired, the *cavaleiro,* who wears 18th century costume, rides out of the ring and the bull is faced by eight *moços de forcado,* who come in on foot, unarmed, in single file to confront the bull. Their leader goes on alone, challenging the beast with loud cries, and when the bull charges the man throws himself at its head and does a handspring on its horns, while the other men grapple with the bull barehanded, and subdue it. These *pegas,* as the rites of the *moços* are called, may have been imported in early times from Greece or Rome, as they much resemble the dances of the sacred bull to be seen on Cretan and Etruscan vases.

Finally, a group of oxen is let into the ring and the bull gallops out with them. Specially brave bulls are kept for breeding, the others are slaughtered for meat. The season lasts from Easter to October. The best fights take place in Lisbon at Campo Pequeno, and in the towns up the Ribatejo where the horses and the bulls are bred.

Fishing and Sailing

Portugal has deep sea fishing all the year round and manned fishing boats are easy to hire in the main fishing ports of Cascais, Sesimbra, Ericeira, Peniche and Nazaré, as well as in the lagoons near Aveiro and all the small ports north of Oporto and those in the Algarve. Sea fishing is also extensively practised from the shore and it is usual to see fishermen with their rods on the sea wall beside the Estrada Marginal from Lisbon to Cascais.

The best freshwater fishing for trout and salmon is in the Minho, Lima and Vouga rivers in the north. Undersea fishing is practised all along the coast, particularly in the lagoons in the Sotavento or eastern end of the Algarve, and in the very deep waters off the Berlenga Islands near Peniche where the *Abrigo para Pescadores,* in an old fort jutting into the sea off Berlenga Grande, has rough accommodation for campers and boats for hire. Sailing is a popular pastime and boats can be hired at many of the beach resorts, as can water-skis and wind-surfers.

Golf

In the Algarve there are several famous championship courses: Penina, between Portimão and Lagos (18 and two 9 holes) was designed by Henry Cotton, as was Vale de Lobo, near Faro, with three distinct 9-hole courses; Vilamoura and Dom Pedro, near Albufeira, (both 18 holes) and Palmares, near Lagos, with five of its 18 holes sited on dunes, are all by Frank Pennick; Quinta do Lago, near Almancil, is an American-designed course of 18 holes. The latest to be opened in the Algarve is the Parque da Floresta at Budens, by the Spaniard Pepé Gancedo. An 18-hole course at Estoril accepts temporary members and the restaurant is open to non-members. There is a very pretty 9-hole course at Linhó on the way to Sintra. The new Quinta da Marinha at Cascais has an 18-hole course designed by Robert Trent Jones, as well as two pools, tennis, riding and a good restaurant. Near Lisbon, at Carregueira, the Lisbon Sports Club has a 9-hole course, and there are others at Miramar and Espinho, near Oporto, Vidago and Vimeiro, as well as in Madeira and the Azores. The one at Troia, on the river Sado opposite Setúbal, also has 18 holes, by Robert Trent Jones.

Shooting
Most shooting in Portugal is free to anyone with a gun and a licence. During the short shooting season in the late autumn, there are areas clearly marked *Regime Florestal,* where no shooting is allowed. Information from the various Tourist Offices.

Tourist Offices

There are Portuguese Tourist Offices in most countries from which you can obtain information and maps. There are no offices in Australia and New Zealand.

Canada: 500 Sherbrooke O. Suite 930, Montreal, PQ H3A 3C6; tel. 514-843-4623.
UK: New Bond House, 1-5 New Bond Street, London W1; tel. 01-493-3873.
USA: 548 Fifth Avenue, New York, NY 10036; tel. 212-354-4403.

Every town of any size in Portugal has a tourist office with brochures and town plans, often in several languages. Details of local buses and trains as well as of coach trips, are available too. The main Tourist offices in Lisbon are in the Palacio Foz, Praça dos Restauradores, 1000 Lisbon (tel. 367031/2/3/4), and Avenida Antonio Augusto de Aguiar 86, 1000 Lisbon, (tel. 575086), and at the Airport.

Castle at Belver

History and Culture

History

Portugal has not changed its frontiers since Afonso Henriques, son of Henry of Burgundy and Teresa, daughter of the King of Leon and Castille, proclaimed himself King of Portucale in 1139 at Guimarães in the north, though it was not until a century later that the Moors were finally driven out of Faro in the extreme south.

From the amount of building and artifacts that remain, it is known that Portugal, with the rest of the Iberian Peninsula, was settled in the Iron Age and Celtic periods. The Greeks and the Phoenicians established trading posts on the coasts and the Romans and the Visigoths both left their marks as did the Moors, who invaded from North Africa in the 8th century.

With the coming of the kingdom in 1139 the chief preoccupation was the fear of Spanish aggression and the victory over the Castillians at Aljubarrota in 1385 gave the country two centuries of calm. The first Treaty of Alliance with England was signed in 1372. The marriage of King John I and Philippa of Lancaster, daughter of John of Gaunt, following the Treaty of Windsor in 1386, cemented the oldest Treaty in the world to be still in force.

The Discoveries
The following century saw Prince Henry the Navigator, third of the sons of King John and Queen Philippa, planning and preparing the voyages of discovery down the coast of Africa, finally rounding Cape Bojador, beyond which the ancients believed that the sea fell into a bottomless abyss. This prepared the way for Columbus to discover America in 1492, for Vasco da Gama to reach India by sea in 1498, Pedro Alvares Cabral to land in Brazil in 1500 and Magellan to circumnavigate the world between 1519 and 1522. These voyages and discoveries resulted in the Portuguese acquisition of their overseas possessions — Angola, Mozambique and Guinea in Africa, Timor and Macau in the Far East, and Brazil. The last named became independent in 1825. Portugal also gained Goa, and a large part of India which went to the British Crown as part of Catherine of Braganza's dowry when she married King Charles II. India annexed Goa in 1961 and the remaining overseas possessions were given their independence in 1975 after the Revolution of 1974, which changed Portugal from being the Corporate State envisaged by Dr Oliveira Salazar, who was in power for almost 40 years, to the present democratically elected President and Government.

The riches that poured into Portugal from Brazil and India in the 16th century and, to a lesser degree, from Africa in the 18th century, enabled the kings and the leading churchmen to indulge in a passion for building, the results of which can be seen today by the fortunate visitor.

Portugal came under Spanish domination from 1580 to 1640, when the Braganzas, a cadet branch of the royal family, led an uprising, turned the Spaniards out of the country and assumed the monarchy, which they retained until the Revolution of 1910.

Peninsular War
The country was invaded during the Napoleonic Wars and Wellington, only later to be created a Duke, led British and Portuguese troops to the victorious Battle of Buçaco against the French in 1810.

A quarter of a century later a civil war between the two sons of King John VI, Dom Pedro and Dom Miguel, ended in 1834 with the exile of Miguel and the death of Pedro. Maria da Glória, Pedro's daughter, became Queen at the age of 15. An expulsion of monks and nuns from their monasteries and convents followed soon after. In the ensuing decades there was much political instability but the religious were gradually allowed to return, though not to their original monasteries which often fell into complete ruin. This instability culminated in the assassination of King Carlos I and his heir in 1908, when they were driving in an open carriage through the streets of Lisbon. He was succeeded by his younger son, Manuel II, who, with his mother, had witnessed the murder of his father and brother. The young Manuel abdicated in 1910 and a Republic was proclaimed.

The Republic
Partly owing to Portugal entering the war of 1914-18 with the Allies against Germany, there were constant political and economic crises. Dr Oliveira Salazar, a Professor of Economics at Coimbra University, was called in, becoming Minister of Finance in 1928 and Head of the Government in 1932. He restored economic stability, kept Portugal out of the Second World War, though allowing Great Britain facilities in the Azores Archipelago after the Treaty of Windsor had been invoked, and retired after a stroke in 1968.

Revolution
Salazar was succeeded as Prime Minister by Dr Marcelo Caetano, a Professor of Law at Lisbon University. But he was not strong enough to continue the dictatorship which Dr Salazar had exercised and was thrown out at the bloodless Carnation Revolution of April 25th, 1974, so called because the soldiers stuck red carnations into the muzzles of their rifles. Since then there have been many changes of government and of President, but a government of Social Democrats has now been voted in by a large majority, inflation is lessening and the majority of the population is more prosperous than ever before.

Refugees from Africa
After independence in Portuguese Africa almost a million men, women and children poured into Portugal from Angola and Mozambique. These *retornados,* or 'returned ones', as they were called, were of every colour and level of education, though they all spoke Portuguese. Thus the country had to absorb about a tenth of her whole population. Today only a very small proportion has not been resettled. Among the latter are many of the Timorense who fled that far eastern island when it was taken over by Indonesia. Few of these speak Portuguese and negotiations are still taking place through the United Nations as to their future.

Culture

Religion
Unlike many other southern European countries, Portugal has for long possessed freedom of religious practice. There have been Anglican churches in Lisbon, Oporto and Funchal, Madeira, since the 18th century, a Scots Church in Lisbon for at least a hundred years and places of worship of many small sects are to be found in most of the larger cities.

Some 90 per cent of Portuguese profess to be Roman Catholics and, since the rise of Fatima as a great international shrine of Our Lady, the numbers of those attending Mass have greatly increased. The people in the north are noticeably more devout than those in the south, where parts of the Alentejo and the Algarve are considered to be mission territory.

The most important artistic manifestations in the country are ecclesiastical or stem from church patronage, as a result of the centuries-old adherence to the Catholic faith. Incidentally the term 'convent' can be used for a religious house of either men or women.

Thus, the fascinating School of Portuguese Primitive painting is almost entirely religious in character.

Architecture
The highly decorated late Gothic style is known as Manueline, after King Manuel I, whose reign of 26 years from 1495 to 1521 saw the opening of the sea routes to Brazil and the Indies. It is almost entirely ecclesiastical, though it derives its inspiration from the Discoveries, using coral, seaweed, ropes, anchors and the armillery sphere, carved in stone as if it were plaster.

The Manueline melted into the Renaissance and, as trade with the Orient increased, Chinese influence was displayed in pottery, china and furniture. The great artistic impulses of Europe reached Portugal considerably later than central Europe and the Baroque and Rococo, with the completely individual twist given to these manifestations by the Portuguese, went on right into the last century.

Although *saudade*, 'yearning', is a characteristic Portuguese word, and the *fados*, the love-sick songs, which are supposed to be so typical of the country, are melancholy, the Portuguese are not a sad or violent race. Their religion, unlike that of the Spaniards, is cheerful and this is particularly shown in the gaiety of Portuguese Baroque. Angels skitter up and down twisted columns, great pictorial panels of glazed blue and white tiles *(azulejos)* line both the interiors and exteriors of churches. In many places houses are also decorated with this fascinating form of art which is peculiar to Portugal. Dutch and Arabic tiles are much smaller and patterned rather than representative.

Domestic building used to vary widely from province to province, but now the country builder seems to have lost the instinctive feeling for harmonious proportion which marked the work of his forebears. However, in the Algarve, the houses are still low and whitewashed with fantastic chimneys; in the Alentejo, the chimneys get wider and the walls are of an even more dazzling white. Further north the cottages are constructed of granite blocks which make the villages sink into the landscape. Oporto is a granite city, whereas Lisbon's houses and apartment blocks are colour-washed in every conceivable shade.

Pottery

There is an abundance of clay for both porcelain and pottery in the country. Lovely porcelain is made at the Vista Alegre works near Aveiro in the Beira Litoral and at Coimbra. The latter city is also a great centre for fine pottery which has been produced there for centuries. The Barcelos cocks in all colours and all sizes are well known, as are the vivid glazed green leaf-shaped plates and dishes from Caldas da Rainha. Other types of pottery come from Alcobaça, Mafra, the Alentejo, where small painted figurines are made, and the Algarve, with traditional Greek and Roman forms of waterpots and jugs still being produced.

Crafts

Other crafts are basket work of all types, carved wooden ox yokes and household utensils, copper and ironwork, and the filigree jewellery made of silver wire and then gold plated.

Lace and embroidery are also traditional crafts. The best-known embroidery comes from Viana do Castelo in the north, with motifs of hearts and flowers, and from Madeira, the Portuguese island in the Atlantic. Arraiolas specialises in hand embroidered wool carpets in many old and modern designs, and Castelo Branco is noted for silk embroidered bedspreads and hangings. Fine tapestries come from Portalegre and linen is hand-woven in the north where flax is grown.

Literature

The three Portuguese writers whose names are widely known abroad are Camões, who wrote the epic poem the *Lusiads* in 1572 commemorating the Discoveries, which has often been translated into English, as well as some lovely sonnets; Eça de Queiroz, the late Victorian novelist, whose books, all of which have been translated into English, are realistic and vividly show the life of the professional classes of his period in Portugal; and, in this century, the poet Fernando Pessoa. Other famous writers are the 16th century Gil Vicente who wrote plays, Almeida Garrett who introduced the Romantic movement into Portugal in the last century and, in more modern times, José Saramago, Aquilino Ribeiro, Miguel Torga, Ferreira de Castro, Fernando Namora, Joaquim Paço d'Arcos, José Lobo Antunes and José Cardoso Pires.

Mills

Windmills, the sails of coarse cotton or linen, reset by the farmer when the whine of the clay whistles on the struts changes and so tells him that the wind has altered, still stand on many hills, particularly in the south and watermills are on the banks of some northern rivers. The old tidal mills up the Tagus have mostly disappeared, as have the *fragatas,* the specially constructed boats which ferried goods across the Tagus before the bridge over the river was built.

Misericordias

Queen Leonor founded the first Misericordias, or Hospitals of Mercy, in the 15th century and these have always been managed by lay bodies of local people. The chapels attached to the old buildings are usually of exceptional interest, containing fine paintings and furnishings. Now that modern hospitals have been built all over the country, the former Misericordias are often used as homes for old people, who are thus able to go on living in their own towns or villages.

Music

The Portuguese are a musical people and sing as they go about their work. Dancing at the country fairs and *romarias* is accompanied by song and almost every town or village of any size has a band. There are no world famous composers, though there were known writers of ecclesiastical music in the 17th and 18th centuries.There is now a revival with a new generation of young composers, several of whom are women.

However, unique to Portugal, is the *Fado.* This is a plaintive ballad, wailed rather than sung, of unrequited love, passion or despair. The *Fadista,* man or woman, wears black in memory of Maria Severa, the most famous and notorious of the early 19th century singers, who died young. The song is accompanied by two guitarists, the audience listens in complete silence and then, when the last strange guttural note is wrung from the tense body of the singer, the response is wildly enthusiastic. Amalia Rodrigues is still the most famous *Fadista* today and her recordings show something of the attraction of this unusual form of art.

Fados can be heard in Lisbon in special restaurants and cafés, though the performance seldom starts before 2200 or 2300. Coimbra, the University town, is another centre, with the students singing together rather than solo as in Lisbon.

Painting and Sculpture

After the flowering of primitive painting in the 15th century, with the great retable of São Vicente by Nuno Gonçalves in the Lisbon Art Museum as its apotheosis, and the work of Frei Carlos in Evora, there were few painters of note. Josefa of Obidos in the 17th century developed a characteristic countryfied style of her own. Then, at the end of the 18th and the beginning of the 19th centuries, Domingos Antonio Sequeira showed by his work that he was a remarkable painter of portraits, family groups and allegorical subjects. He also designed the splendid gold-plated table service which a grateful Portuguese government presented to the Duke of Wellington after the Peninsular War. This is on show in Apsley House in London.

History and Culture

Towards the end of the last century, the leading painter was Columbano Bordalo Pinheiro, whose admirable portraits can be seen in the Contemporary Art Museum in Lisbon. A little later there was Almada Negreiros while Vieira da Silva, who became a French national, is widely known for her abstracts. Other contemporary painters of note are Paula Rego, Julio Pomar and José Guimarães.

Possibly owing to the wealth of stone and marble to be found in the country, there are many remarkable sculptures in Portugal, beginning with the unique Iron Age idol, the Colossus of Pedralva, in Guimarães. The Gothic tombs in Coimbra, Lisbon Cathedral and the 14th century sarcophagi of D. Pedro and Inez at Alcobaça are memorable, as are the carved stone retables in many northern churches. Machado de Castro, in the 18th century, produced the great bronze equestrian statue of King José I in Lisbon's waterfront square and a host of delightful polychrome wood and terracotta figures of the country people of his time, as well as of saints. In the last century, Soares dos Reis was the leading sculptor and his work can be seen in the museum that bears his name in Oporto. Lagoa Henriques and José Cutileiro are the best known sculptors of the present day.

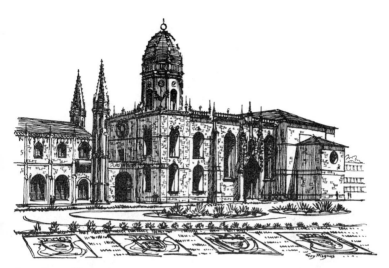

Jeronimos Monastery

Lisbon

The capital of Portugal, with around a million inhabitants, is spread in a wide semi-circle on a number of hills on the banks of the river Tagus. The Tagus is a great river by the time it reaches Lisbon and the Atlantic ocean; ever since the Greeks traded along the coasts of the Iberian peninsula it has been a lifeline for Lisbon.

It is believed that the Phoenicians formed a trading settlement here. Then the Romans arrived, fortified the hill on which St George's castle now stands and left traces of their occupation all over the country. They gave Lisbon the name of *Felicita Julia,* built roads out of the city and municipal buildings within it. After the Romans withdrew from the peninsula the Visigoths strengthened the fortifications and, after conversion to Christianity, built the first cathedral below the Castle hill.

Next the Moors poured in from Spain and called the city *'Olissibona',* adorning it with buildings, none of which now remains, though traces of the Moorish domination are to be found in place names. These mostly begin with 'Al', not only in Lisbon itself, such as Alcantara, one of the valleys leading to the river, and Alfama, still largely a medieval part of the city, but all over the southern part of the country.

Lisbon

The Moors tolerated the Christians, but in 1147 ships with English, German and Flemish Crusaders, who were sailing to the Holy Land, were driven ashore near Oporto by a great storm. The first King of Portugal, Afonso Henriques, who was only in possession of the northern part of the country, persuaded them to sail on south and drive the Moors out of Lisbon.

City Centre

By the mid-13th century the court was settled in Lisbon and then, as now, the Rossio was the centre of the city. It is a fine square with the National Theatre on the north side and surrounded by the formal 18th century houses which the Marques of Pombal, then Prime Minister, built after the great earthquake of 1755. The streets leading from the Rossio to the riverside arcaded square of the Praça do Comercio are all designed on a grid pattern with these beautiful houses on either side — an early example of town planning. The Rua do Ouro, as its name implies, was the goldsmiths' street, the Rua da Prata, the silversmiths', and the Rua Augusta, now a pedestrian precinct, leads down to a triumphal arch giving on to the Praça do Comercio. These streets are lined with banks and good shops, for it is the original commercial section of the city. There are other excellent shops and shopping centres in all the residential parts around the Parque Eduardo VII, at the top of the Avenida da Liberdade, and in the apartment blocks on the way to the airport.

In the centre of the Praça do Comercio is the great equestrian bronze statue of Dom José I designed by Machado de Castro. The King, in a breastplate and plumed helmet, astride a splendid horse, has now weathered to a lovely green. Long ago, when the statue was still bronze coloured, the great space was named Black Horse Square by English visitors; and before the assassination of King Carlos I and his elder son in 1908 at the north-west corner of this square in front of the General Post Office, it was called Terreiro do Paço, Palace Yard, as the Royal palace was here up to the 18th century and Catherine of Braganza sailed from this spot to England for her marriage to Charles II.

As has been indicated already, Lisbon is essentially an 18th century city, for the great earthquake of 1755, and the tidal wave which followed it, destroyed the whole of the lower part of the town. However, the Castle which rises on a hill to the east and the Cathedral below it, still stand, as do many 17th century houses in the Alfama district around the Cathedral. Another early part is the Bairro Alto, on a hill to the west of the Avenida da Liberdade.

Lovers of *art nouveau* will delight in the number of apartment houses, and even shop fronts, built in the first 20 to 30 years of this century which are to be found all over the city. The office blocks and apartments of the past 35 years mostly have a dignity which you do not find in many other countries, for the door and window surrounds are all of stone or marble and the façades are colour-washed in pastel tones of pink, blue, green or cream, and there are pots of geraniums and other flowering plants on every balcony. Unhappily the local architects have recently decided to be original at all costs. Thus the appearance of the city around the main Avenida da Liberdade has completely changed with the building of office blocks, glass-fronted or violently coloured in vivid tomato red, mustard yellow and even black.

Buses and trams run all over Lisbon and are very reasonable in price. Stopping places are marked by a sign *'Paragem'*. Books of 20 tickets, at half the price charged on the vehicle, can be bought outside Cais do Sodré Station and other terminals. The underground has a flat fare rate.

St George's Castle
The much-restored St George's castle can be reached either by a bus which starts in the Rossio, a taxi, or by walking uphill past the cathedral. There is no entrance fee and the visitor reaches a wide battlemented grassed space with fine old trees. The view is superb over the centre of the city, with the Rossio and the Praça do Comercio below, the great river which widens above Lisbon into what is called the 'Sea of Straw'. From the top of any of the castle towers one can also see the Sintra hills and, in the middle distance, the suspension bridge, one of the longest in Europe, thrown across the Tagus some twenty-five years ago.

Wandering around the castle lawns are flocks of white birds — ducks, geese, swans and turkeys; stone benches are provided and tables for picnics. There is also an excellent and expensive restaurant serving lunches — the Casa do Leão.

Between the inner and the outer walls of the castle, there is a largely medieval village with narrow lanes winding between houses, still lived in by local artisans. In the centre is a charming, formal square with benches shaded by plane trees and the church of the Holy Cross at one side. In this square at number 5, Michel's is a luxury French restuarant.

The Cathedral and the Alfama
In Portugal, a cathedral is called the Sé (like the See of a bishopric in England), and if a visitor asks for directions to get to the cathedral, he will not be understood. The Lisbon Sé was begun in 1150 and much restored through the centuries. The interior is noble and the renaissance chancel, with a lovely 18th century organ at one side, has not been altered. The chapels behind the high altar contain splendid Gothic tombs, including one of a woman reading a book with two dogs fighting at her feet. Beyond these are the somewhat

derelict cloisters with a fine 13th century iron screen to one of the chapels. The font in the cathedral is that in which St Anthony of Padua was baptised in 1195, and it is nice to think of the babies of the parish being christened in the same stone basin. The saint was born in a house opposite the main door of the cathedral and later on a small Italianate-looking church, Santo António da Sé, was built over the spot.

Further up the hill from the cathedral, a public garden to the right gives a bird's eye view of the roofs and narrow alleyways of the Alfama district, which is well worth exploring on foot, with its medieval houses and glimpses of flowering trees through grilled apertures set in high walls.

Espirito Santo Foundation
The way up goes on to the Fundação Ricardo Espirito Santo Silva. This is a museum and school of the decorative arts in which young men and women are trained in many rare handicrafts, such as book binding, the application of gold leaf, repairing antique carpets, wood carving, ormolu, sculpture and cabinet making to such a high degree of perfection that the copies of 18th century furniture are all marked with a special cipher to show that they are not genuine, and cannot therefore be sold as antiques by unscrupulous dealers. There are over 20 workshops, each devoted to a different aspect of the decorative arts and this remarkable foundation also runs a course for interior decorators, thus keeping alive the long Portuguese tradition of fine craftsmanship.

Summer Festivities
It is in and around this old part of Lisbon, stretching down from the castle to the docksides, that the local people make merry on the nights of the feast days of the three patrons of Lisbon, St Anthony on June 12th/13th, St John on the 23rd/24th and St Peter on the 28th/29th. Strings of coloured paper hang across the streets, young people dance to the wild music of the local bands, and dances are held in all the covered markets of Lisbon when the fun goes on all night. Little booths sell sizzling fresh sardines, grilled over charcoal and glasses of strong red wine.

Flea Market
On the hill up river, to the east of the castle, behind the great Italianate church of São Vicente, Lisbon's Flea Market, *Feira da Ladra,* is held every Tuesday and Saturday in the Campo de Sta Clara. But it is now rare to find a bargain there, as it is in the antique shops in the Rua do Alecrim, the Rua da Escola Politécnica and the Rua de São Bento.

Braganza Pantheon
Off the cloisters at the side of the São Vicente church, is the Braganza Pantheon with the stone coffins of all the later Kings and Queens of

The Jeronimos Church, Lisbon, famous for its carved stonework.

View over the Alfama quarter of Lisbon and the River Tagus from the Castelo de S. Jorge.

One of the beaches near Albufeira on the Algarve coast.

The Praço do Comercio facing the Tagus in central Lisbon. The statue is of Dom José I.